Original title:
Laughs Lost in the Larch

Copyright © 2025 Creative Arts Management OÜ
All rights reserved.

Author: Thomas Sinclair
ISBN HARDBACK: 978-1-80567-458-0
ISBN PAPERBACK: 978-1-80567-757-4

Embers of Cheer in Gloomy Places

In a forest where shadows play tricks,
The trees wear their humor like old silly flicks.
Squirrels throw acorns like jesters in flight,
While the mushrooms just giggle, hidden from sight.

The owls hoot in riddles, all wise and profound,
As the shadows stretch long, dancing round and round.
A rabbit in bowtie pretends to be grand,
In a world full of mirth, just bursting with sand.

Crickets are chirping their slapstick refrain,
While the puddles reflect all the joy and the pain.
The wind tells a tale, it tickles the leaves,
As the laughter of breezes is all that it weaves.

In this woodland of whimsy, where giggles ignite,
And tall tales unravel in the pale silver light.
Every nook holds a chuckle, each path speaks in rhyme,
Where the playful heart wanders, transcending all time.

Shadows of Glee

In a grove where giggles roam,
Trees sway like they've found a home.
Bouncing whispers, chasing light,
Wobbly shapes in breezy flight.

Squirrels chuckle at the scene,
Twisting branches, leafy green.
Oh, to dance in a dreamlike trance,
As shadows twist into a prance.

Faded Laughter under Canopy

Beneath the branches wide and tall,
Echoes of mirth began to fall.
Sunshine giggles, soft and rare,
Lost in leaves, they drift in air.

We gathered stories, wild and strange,
As rain turned smiles to sweet exchange.
Those moments stowed in nature's chest,
Where joy retreats, but never rests.

Memories Adrift in the Pines

Pine needles quilt the forest floor,
With whispers of past tales galore.
A jester's hat, a tickling breeze,
Oh how the woodland used to tease!

Through knotted roots and shadows cast,
We reminisce on the laughs amassed.
Though time may fade the merry song,
The forest hums where we belong.

The Silence of Ticklish Days

In the hush of an emerald glade,
Where giggles dance but never fade.
A gentle breeze stirs playful sighs,
Under the vast, unseeing skies.

We chased the sun, embraced the mirth,
Each silly stumble weighed with worth.
Yet silence grows amidst the fun,
A quiet memory, but never done.

Cackles Carried by the Wind

When a squirrel prances, all dressed in grey,
It flips its tail, in a cheeky display.
A peace offering tossed, then forgotten,
Leaves us grinning, while the moment's begotten.

A loud crackle, a branch starts to sway,
Landing on someone whose laughter won't stay.
Rolling on the ground, what a sight to behold,
While the breeze weaves the stories we've told.

Frayed Threads of Hilarity

In the attic, where old jokes breathe,
Dusty laughter's woven in each frayed sleeve.
A favorite hat takes quite the fall,
Dancing like a clown, it hangs on the wall.

Nostalgia tugs, with a subtle grin,
Two clowns play tug-o-war; none will win.
Every slip and trip becomes a delight,
As echoes of chuckles rise into the night.

Dreams of Merriment in Solitude

A lone dog barks at an imaginary friend,
Each woof a giggle, that never will end.
Socks on the floor dance undermoonlight,
Whirling together, while the shadows take flight.

Through the window, a melody drifts,
A tune of mischief, as thoughtfulness shifts.
Alone in the stillness, I chuckle alone,
For every wobbly note feels like homegrown.

Echoing Lameness in Larches

The trees whisper secrets of clumsy feats,
As roots trip the light in their playful beats.
A squirrel drops down with a fumble and spin,
It shakes its head, then tumbles again.

The wind chimes with tales of blunders so grand,
As echoes of laughter spread wide through the land.
Each silly mishap layered in fun,
We gather the giggles, our joy weighs a ton.

Memories Woven in Wood

Beneath the branches, whispers play,
Where giggles hide and dare to sway.
A squirrel trips on a branch so thin,
And laughter bursts where woes begin.

The knots in trunks tell tales so bold,
Of laughter shared as stories unfold.
We gathered round with hearts so light,
While shadows danced in fading light.

Wistful Mirth beneath the Leaves

A rustling leaf, a silly shout,
Echoes of joy, a playful bout.
Elusive giggles float through the air,
As if the trees believe they're fair.

Mushrooms sprout in a comical line,
With gnarled roots that twist and twine.
In every creak, a chuckle is found,
Nature's jesters all around.

Chasing Giggles Through the Glade

Amid the ferns, we chase a sound,
With every step, more joy is found.
The sunlight flickers in playful guise,
And mischief dances in green eyes.

A wobbly rabbit hops with flair,
While we dive into the soft, cool air.
In gleeful bounds, we search for glee,
Among the trunks and blissful spree.

Silences Between the Boughs

Where hush surrounds, a chuckle sneaks,
In secret nooks, our laughter peaks.
Branches sway with unheard delight,
While we recount the silliest sight.

In stillness held, our hearts embrace,
The echoes of joy leave naught a trace.
Yet in our smiles, the moments stay,
A timeless jest in nature's play.

Charmed Yet Unseen

In the woods where whispers gleam,
Squirrels dance with silly dreams.
Branches sway like giggling sprites,
Beneath the moon, they play all night.

Beneath the boughs, a chuckle hides,
A rabbit in a top hat bides.
They swap their tales of fleeting glee,
Oh, how they wish for company!

Leaves rustle with a quiet jest,
Tickling thoughts that never rest.
Beneath the shade, they keep it fun,
A world where laughter's never done.

Traces of Tittering in Twilight

As shadows stretch and twilight falls,
The crickets hum their silly calls.
The owls wink with a jest so sly,
While fireflies blink a cheeky eye.

With each rustle, the trees conspire,
Creating tales that never tire.
A fox in stripes, a sight so rare,
Adds mischief to the evening air.

The brook chuckles, a playful friend,
Telling secrets that never end.
While all around, the night is bright,
With traces of glee in soft moonlight.

The Sigh of the Silenced Wood

The trees may stand so tall and grand,
Yet inside, a giggle's planned.
Across the ground, where shadows creep,
Lies a squirrel with secrets to keep.

With whispers lost to fading light,
The woods would chuckle if in sight.
A pinecone falls with comical grace,
And laughter echoes through this space.

Though silence wraps the grove in gloom,
A playful heart will find its room.
For in the hush, a charm remains,
Where funny flits like falling rains.

Nods to the Nostalgic Nook

In the corner where memories lay,
Old giggles dance in bright array.
A bottle cap, a yo-yo spins,
Each trinket sings of childish wins.

Upon the bench, where shadows merge,
The echoes of laughter gently surge.
With every tease and cheeky poke,
The past embraces each little joke.

Beneath the branches, mossy and sweet,
The stories twist, they wiggle, they greet.
In this nook, the heart finds cheer,
A timeless space, forever near.

Whispers of What Once Was

In a garden where giggles bloomed,
Echoes of joy now softly fumed.
Once bright with tricks and playful schemes,
Now shrouded in soft, forgotten dreams.

Beneath the branches, shadows prance,
Where silly whispers used to dance.
A squirrel snickers, his secret spree,
While we recall what used to be.

The breeze teases with past delight,
As sunbeams chuckle, oh what a sight.
In every rustle, a jest retold,
Yet here we stand, both brave and bold.

But as we wander, hearts aflame,
Good old mirth calls us by name.
With every step, a tender trace,
Reminds us laughter has its place.

Hidden Smirks in the Shadows

In twilight's haze, mischief hides,
With quirky tales and playful tides.
A whisper tickles the ears of time,
Where sneaker games used to prime.

The moonlight spins a funny yarn,
As shadows dance on the old barn.
Every chuckle, a ghostly play,
Bringing back those joyous days.

Behind tall trees, where secrets brew,
A band of squirrels in a goofy crew.
Chasing fireflies, they plot and schem,
Reminding us life was once a dream.

Yet in the dark, a smirk we find,
These little giggles are still entwined.
In corners where the laughter grew,
Whispers of joy, still shining through.

Echoes of the Unexpressed

In the quiet woods, thoughts are stilled,
Yet hidden chuckles wait, fulfilled.
Each branch holds stories half-untold,
Of silly pranks brave, and bold.

The leaves rustle with unspent glee,
Where once we frolicked wild and free.
With every creak of ancient wood,
Comes the punchline of what once could.

Echoing tales that tickle the mind,
Of slippery slopes and winds unkind.
We trudge through paths that make us grin,
Recalling all the mischief within.

In every nook, a playful muse,
Whispers of joy we dare not lose.
Though laughter fades into the dusk,
The echoes remain, a fragrant husk.

Fray of the Forgotten Frolic

Beneath the larches, memories hide,
Of hearty laughs and unplanned rides.
A brook chuckles, as it goes by,
Reminding us of days gone awry.

In the weeds where tricks took flight,
The stars above still twinkle bright.
Those days are frayed, like an old coat,
Yet whispers of fun continue to float.

A tumble here, a splatter there,
Each moment draped in light and flair.
We chase the breeze with open hearts,
While the past tickles, and the present starts.

The squirrels giggle from heights above,
Fueling the warmth of forgotten love.
In every memory, a spark ignites,
A playful reminder of starry nights.

Fading Folly into the Fir Trees

Whispers of giggles drift in the breeze,
Swaying branches with playful tease.
A squirrel stumbles, slips on a pine,
Makes all the forest share a laugh divine.

Frogs in a chorus, croaking with flair,
A rubber chicken dances, without a care.
The wind carries jokes from trunk to trunk,
Every tree holds a secret, every branch a funk.

Beneath the spread of a grand old tree,
Hiccups of humor float wild and free.
A pinecone pitches, a giggle ensues,
While shadows of silliness spread in hues.

Laughter once echoed, now whispers remain,
Yet the spirit of whimsy will ever sustain.
With each rustle of leaves, they still hum,
Nature's own jesters, forever fun.

Tattered Dreams of Delighted Echoes

Dreams once vibrant now frayed round the edges,
Whimsical echoes from forest's ledges.
A jester's hat tangled high on a bough,
Tickles the branches, prompting a wow!

Raccoons in masks plot mischief at night,
Chasing their shadows, what a funny sight!
With fleeting folly as clouds drift by,
The moon chuckles softly, a celestial spy.

Tickled trees giggle, their gnarled backs cry,
As sparrows bring tales from high in the sky.
A tumble of leaves, a comical leap,
Nestled in laughter, the forest shall keep.

Though dreams get tattered, they never fade,
Echoing joy in the glades once played.
A snapshot of whimsy, a flash in the air,
Just close your eyes tight, it's lingering there.

Scribbles of Laughter on Bark

Marks of delight carved on aged bark,
Tell tales of laughter that once left a mark.
A beaver, unsteady, builds quite the raft,
While woodland creatures all giggle and laugh.

Jokes written in sap, secrets in rings,
Whispers of joy that a free spirit brings.
Dancing shadows play games in the sun,
As nature chuckles, oh, isn't it fun?

Nutty acorns drop with a thud and a bounce,
Squirrels all scatter, wearing their crowns.
The echoes of jests join in the fray,
Each tickling moment brightens the day.

With bark as the canvas, fun knows no end,
In the woods of folly, there's laughter to send.
Pine-scented joy hung in the air,
Crafted by woodland's creative flair.

Tender Chasms of Forgotten Glee

In the dappled grove of old verdant trees,
Gentle echoes whisper on the soft breeze.
Chasms of cheer once danced in the light,
Now hidden in shadows, retreating from sight.

A tumbleweed giggles, rolls down the path,
While coyotes snicker and share in the laugh.
Moss-covered stones hold fables of fun,
Stories of sparkles beneath the warm sun.

A wren in her nest, with a playful squawk,
Pokes fun at the world with each cheeky talk.
Memories linger, though moments may fade,
In the heart of the woods, mischief is made.

Though the laughter has softened like whispers of air,
These tender chasms hold humor beyond compare.
For in every rustle, in every soft plea,
Joy echoes back from the roots of the trees.

The Haunting of Playful Spirits

In twilight's glow, the spirits play,
With whispers soft, they dance and sway.
A tickle here, a giggle there,
In moonlit pranks, they bring good cheer.

Beneath the trees where shadows creep,
Their jests awake from slumber deep.
A flicker, a flutter, a sudden shout,
They tease the night, laughing about.

In corners dark, the mischief grows,
With every bark, their laughter flows.
An echo of joy, a sound so light,
Playful spirits reign in the night.

So heed the call of the giggling air,
For cheeky phantoms linger near.
In every rustle, a jest unfolds,
Their playful hearts, a treasure yet untold.

Specters of Jests Beneath Starlight

Under the stars where shadows glide,
The spirits of fun take joyful ride.
With every twinkle, a chuckle spins,
The dance of mischief surely begins.

Among the leaves, the whispers creep,
A hidden giggle that won't let sleep.
A snap and a rustle, the night feels bright,
As jests weave tales in silver light.

Echoes of laughter fill the trees,
In breezes soft, they tease and squeeze.
With twirls and jumps, they paint the ground,
In every corner, delight is found.

Chase them away? Oh, never so,
These jolly spirits bring the glow.
In their presence, worries cease,
For laughter's magic brings sweet peace.

Footprints of Happiness in the Soil

Where laughter danced like petals do,
Footprints remain in morning dew.
Each mark a story of joy and fun,
Adventures shared 'til night is done.

A wiggle here, a skip in time,
Each playful step, a laughter chime.
Through winding paths and grassy knolls,
The echoes linger in our souls.

With every trace, a memory glows,
Of silly antics that everyone knows.
In the quiet earth, mirth takes root,
Reminding us joy is absolute.

So stroll the ground where echoes play,
Embrace the light of yesterday.
For in the soil, those laughs persist,
A twist of fate we can't resist.

Jaded Chuckles Against the Bark

The trees wear laughter like a grin,
As chuckles hang in the air like sin.
With every roughness of the trunk,
A hidden jest in the mossy funk.

The branches sway, the leaves conspire,
In whispered tones, they spark the fire.
A snicker flies from oak to pine,
As jaded giggles intertwine.

Against the bark, the humor sticks,
With every knock, a new surprise clicks.
In nature's arms, we find delight,
A tapestry of laughs in the night.

So pause and breathe where these trees stand,
For playful spirits sweep the land.
In jaded chuckles, we find our way,
To the heart of joy that's here to stay.

Breezes Carrying Cheery Echoes

In a forest where whispers play,
The branches dance, oh what a display!
Squirrels chortle, chipmunks cheer,
Their silly antics draw us near.

The shadows bounce with a clang and a clatter,
A riddle here, a puzzle that matters.
Frogs sing out in a croaky tune,
While fireflies twirl beneath the moon.

Branches sway with a jovial sway,
Telling tales of a prankster's day.
The rustling leaves in fits of glee,
Hold secrets of laughter 'neath each tree.

As we stumble through this giggly glade,
In nature's show, our worries fade.
With every step, the spirits cheer,
In breezes carrying joy so clear.

Ghosts of Giggles Amidst the Trees

Underneath the boughs so wide,
Whimsy rides on the gentle tide.
Echoes linger like playful banshees,
Whispering chuckles among the leaves.

A wobbly owl begins to hoot,
While squirrels throw acorns in hot pursuit.
The sun winks down with a cheeky grin,
As shadows play where giggles begin.

In hiding spots, the fairies peek,
With hands on mouths, they hardly speak.
Their laughter bubbles, an eerie sound,
In every nook where fun is found.

Gone but not lost, those laughs we chase,
In every corner of this merry place.
With every rustle, a phantom prance,
Inviting all to join the dance.

Mirthful Mists in the Groves

Fog rolls gently, a soft embrace,
Hiding giggles in its lace.
A rabbit hops, a grin so wide,
Through tickling grass it does abide.

The misty morning hides a jest,
Where silly footsteps know no rest.
With every twist and shout of glee,
The trees lean in, they want to see.

Chipmunks peek from mossy beds,
With tiny paws and sun-kissed heads.
The world is bright where laughter grows,
In mists that dance where the warm wind blows.

As daylight breaks, the antics thrive,
A secret nook where joy's alive.
With boundless fun, we take our cue,
Amidst the mist, we frolic anew.

Remnants of Raucous Revelry

Once the sun dipped low with flair,
A party bloomed in the fragrant air.
Laughter echoed through the night,
While merry spirits took to flight.

The daisies chuckled, the grass wore a grin,
In tangled roots where we began.
With every stomp, a dance profound,
Our joy scattered all around.

But dawn approached with a sleepy sigh,
And scattered giggles began to fly.
Every shadow held a trace,
Of laughter's warmth, its bright embrace.

Yet still we linger, as echoes say,
In every rustle, in every sway.
The remnants of fun still hang around,
In every tree where joy is found.

The Chill of Absent Laughter

In the grove where whispers roam,
Echoes dance, yet feel like foam.
Jokes once flew like birds in flight,
Now they linger, out of sight.

Where are all the giggles bright?
Buried deep in shadows' bite.
Pranks and puns, now tales of yore,
Left the trees to sigh and bore.

Tickling winds seek jesters' cheer,
But silence wraps what used to steer.
A pie in face, all splat and gleam,
Now just whispers in a dream.

So I sit beneath these boughs,
Missing laughs and playful cows.
Nature's humor, lost in haze,
Craves a spark of lively days.

Serenades of Forgotten Fun

In the shade of tall sweet pines,
Humor tickles, never fines.
But the bottles of mirth now dry,
Leaves a thought: oh, how they fly!

Remembering the pie fights bold,
And the tales that never get old.
Yet the wind just croons alone,
A lonesome tune, a weary tone.

Bubbles burst without a sound,
Once we laughed all around.
Now the glades are bittersweet,
With echoes of a skipped heartbeat.

The serenade of giggles fades,
As shadows creep, the light invades.
Beneath the stars, we danced in jest,
Now the night feels like a test.

Lamenting Over Lost Festivity

Once there were balloons of cheer,
Now the air feels far too sheer.
Confetti dreams that filled the night,
Muffled whispers of delight.

Board games stacked, a dusty pile,
Strategy lost, and not a smile.
A dance of joy, now just a shuffle,
As memories fade, we lose the ruffle.

When laughter painted skies with glee,
Now a canvas, bland to see.
Slides and swings once held great charm,
Now they wait, devoid of warm.

Oh, the jesters have gone away,
Left behind an empty play.
In every grove where fun once thrived,
Silence reigns where joy arrived.

The Weight of Smiles Gone

In the park where laughter lay,
Sunshine's glow has lost its sway.
Chasing joy down winding trails,
Mirth now buried, scarce it pales.

The picnic cloth remains unfurled,
No clinking cups in laughter's world.
Just shadows dance under the tree,
Where smiles once roamed wild and free.

Echoes of our playful cheer,
Now only whispers linger near.
Ticklish winds no longer tease,
A tinge of loss in every breeze.

Wondering where the jesters fled,
Each thought feels heavy, tinged with dread.
The spaces where our joy should swell,
Now harbor tales we cannot tell.

Buried Grins Among the Roots

Underneath where shadows creep,
Old giggles hide, not making a peep.
They've tangled up with twigs and leaves,
Chasing squirrels, like playful thieves.

In the soil, a chuckle brews,
Tickled by the morning dews.
Forgotten jokes, deep down they stay,
Whispering tales of yesterday.

Roots wrap tight, they hold their jest,
Secrets nestled in nature's chest.
Buried grins, a cheeky sprout,
Rolling laughter, there's no doubt.

When the breeze begins to tease,
Echoes of mirth dance through the trees.
In each rustle, a giggle glints,
Finding joy where the wildbird flints.

The Gloom Behind the Green

In shadows deep where leaves entwine,
Frolics hide, sipping pickle brine.
Gloomy spots where shadows play,
Pine cones chuckle, in their own way.

The branches bend with tales askew,
Jokes that no one ever knew.
In the quiet, fun takes flight,
Masked by foliage, out of sight.

A toadstool draped in mystery,
Hums of humor, but never a spree.
Beneath the gloom, laughter flows,
A playful breeze where mischief grows.

Behind the green, the smiles loom,
Waiting to burst like a flower's bloom.
In each dark nook, a jest may croon,
Whispers of joy beneath the moon.

Faded Frolics in the Foliage

Worn leaves crinkle, tales of glee,
Time and laughter in harmony.
Whiskered memories flutter down,
Like jolly clowns, without a frown.

In the underbrush, a cackle stirs,
Chasing sunbeams like fluttering birds.
Each rustling leaf a voice of cheer,
Echoes of fun we long to hear.

The canopy holds a tickled scream,
Hidden giggles amidst the dream.
Faded frolics in shades of green,
Nature's jests that go unseen.

Swaying branches, in laughter steep,
Whispers from the woods, secrets they keep.
In every nook where shadows dwell,
Dancing light and tales to tell.

Muffled Merriments in the Maple

Deep in the canopy, secrets sway,
Muffled merriment joins the play.
Maple leaves giggle with the sun,
Hiding smiles, making fun.

Twisting roots in a playful trick,
Tapping rhythms, a whispered flick.
The squirrels' chatter, a giggling spree,
In every whir, a hidden glee.

Branches sway like laughter strong,
Each rustle hums a merry song.
Under the boughs, a silly jest,
Nature's chuckles, at their best.

When the wind stirs up the trees,
Laughter mingles with the breeze.
In the maple, joy does twine,
Muffled moments, oh so fine.

The Humor That Faded in the Grove

In the grove where giggles thrived,
Ticklish whispers had arrived.
But the echoes turned to sighs,
As fun slipped through like butterflies.

Chirping birds told jokes of old,
Witty tales, both brave and bold.
Yet silence crept with feet so light,
Leaving shadows where laughs took flight.

We danced beneath the towering trees,
With pranks done up with greater ease.
But their branches now hold still,
No more tricks, just echoes chill.

Mirth once bloomed like wildflower fields,
Now only memory gently yields.
A chuckle lost among the bark,
Where joy once danced, it's now gone dark.

Mischief among the Evergreens

In the pines, a scheme took shape,
With clever minds as the escapes.
A squirrel's jest, a rabbit's grin,
But now those giggles wear thin.

Underneath the prickly shade,
Laughter rang like a masquerade.
Now the wind just whispers low,
Where once the playful moments flowed.

The trickster fox, with eyes so bright,
Would spin a yarn by morning light.
But now he walks with quiet grace,
No tomfoolery in that space.

The shadows loom, no shadows gleam,
Laughter lost like a broken dream.
Through the branches, sighs now flit,
Where mischief lived, the silence sits.

Beneath the Boughs of Laughter

Beneath the branches, giggles fell,
With stories spun like a spell.
But time turned days to dusky nights,
And quiet claimed the vibrant sights.

The forest floor once paved with fun,
Now holds traces of days undone.
A game of hide, a playful chase,
But now the boughs wear a somber face.

The critters laughed with glee each day,
Played hopscotch on the sunlit hay.
Yet whispers shroud the jovial air,
Where joy was rich, now silence bare.

The echoes fade, yet still we try,
To kindle sparks where the stories lie.
But beneath the branches, the jokes grow old,
With memories trapped in the boughs so cold.

When Smiles Turned to Silence

When smiles danced among the leaves,
Each twinkle worn like autumn sheaves.
Yet clouds rolled in with thunderous frowns,
Dimming hues from vibrant towns.

A jester pranced with antics bright,
But ended up in an empty light.
The chuckles lost, a muted tune,
Forgotten echoes beneath the moon.

Chatter spilled from every side,
But now the whispers look to hide.
From vibrant hues to shadows' clutch,
The fun diminished—oh, what a touch!

Where once the air buzzed, now is meek,
A silence sculpted, small and bleak.
Yet in the stillness, echoes play,
In lost smiles that drift away.

Woodland Echoes of Yesteryears

In the woods where old jokes play,
Squirrels dance in a light-hearted way.
Trees giggle with secrets untold,
As whispers of laughter drift, bold.

Mushrooms chuckle, donning their hats,
While shadows of jesters engage in spats.
The brook burbles with tales of delight,
As echoes of humor take graceful flight.

Leaves flutter, a comedy of grace,
Each fluttering twist, a mischievous face.
Nature composes its jesters anew,
In the light of the sun, laughter shines through.

From mossy corners, a snicker runs wide,
Where playful tomfoolery tries to hide.
A rustle reveals a raccoon in glee,
As woodland wonders share their decree.

Hidden Humors in the Underbrush

Beneath the ferns, a giggle does bloom,
Tiny creatures create quite the room.
A hedgehog wears glasses too large for his size,
As the snickers of frogs take to the skies.

In the thicket, a chuckle unfolds,
With tales of adventures that never get old.
A squirrel tells stories of acorns gone wild,
While the branches sway, like a mischief-filled child.

The brook runs with laughter, so light and so free,
Each splash a reminder of whimsy's decree.
Butterflies waltz through the shimmering air,
Spreading the jests like a blossoming flare.

In patches of sunlight, the humor runs rife,
With a breeze that tickles, bringing things to life.
A delightful sense of play, never a bore,
As the woods hold their secrets, forever in store.

Flickering Smirks in the Pines

In the pines, where the shadows grow long,
A melody of whispers, sweet like a song.
Woodpeckers tap out a rhythmic delight,
As earthworms chuckle beneath the moonlight.

Each breeze brings a story, a moment to share,
With the wind weaving laughter through the air.
A playful fox winks with a curl of his tail,
As the trees stand still, cloaked in their veil.

Mice scamper and whisper of things that they've seen,
Underneath mushrooms, a whimsical scene.
Fireflies twinkle with mirth in their glow,
As shadows unite in a jubilant show.

In the heart of the forest, where whimsy runs wild,
A symphony of giggles from nature's own child.
As pine cones tumble, laughter ensues,
Creating a tapestry of clever ruse.

The Cradle of Abandoned Joy

In a glade where the lost giggles play,
Old toys whisper tales of sunlit days.
A teddy bear with a button for eye,
Joins the chorus of laughter that flits by.

Rusting tricycles and swings filled with dust,
Cradle memories of joy, once robust.
Squirrels recall every tumble and fall,
While echoing spirits in shadows enthrall.

Under the gaze of a wise old pine,
The remnants of humor in each playful line.
Forgotten delights weave soft in the breeze,
As daisies stand tall, bringing smiles to knees.

So gather the giggles from past's gentle reach,
In this cradle of joy where the spirits all preach.
Nature's own laughter is forever our friend,
Hiding in memories that never will end.

Retreating Joys in Twilight

In twilight's grip, the shadows prance,
Giggles hide, they take a chance.
The fireflies wink with mischievous glee,
As whispers of fun dance wild and free.

Beneath the trees, where secrets creep,
A ticklish breeze makes the silence leap.
Moonbeams chuckle, the night teases play,
While mischief lurks where the shadows sway.

Whimsies Adrift on Forest Air

Pinecones tumble like silly clowns,
Squirrels cartwheel in playful rounds.
The brook babbles jokes, no one can hear,
As laughter escapes through the bending spear.

A jester's cap sits on a branch,
Nature's comedy, a daring chance.
In every rustle, a giggle is spun,
Whimsical echoes of forest fun.

Traces of Playfulness Amidst Timbers

Amongst the trunks where shadows grow,
Traces of joy leave a playful glow.
A rabbit hops in his bowtie attire,
While trees lean close, as if to conspire.

The air is thick with laughter's scent,
Each rustling leaf a fun-filled event.
It's a merry race, a chase in disguise,
Where time stands still, and whimsy flies.

Enigmas of Joy and Wilderness

What secret jests the wild things weave?
Puzzles of joy the forest leaves.
Beneath the boughs, the giggles blend,
With riddles that twist around every bend.

The owls hoot out a cheeky grain,
While shadows engage in a silly game.
In the heart of the wild, where laughter spins,
Joy finds a way to sneak back in.

The Vanishing Grin

A jester hung his hat on a tree,
With leaves that danced as they pleased,
A squirrel stole a crown, oh me!
While birds laughed, quite unpleased.

The echoes of giggles fade out fast,
As shadows play tricks on the ground,
Pine cones tumble down, steadfast,
The humor's lost, none abound.

Yet in the breeze, a chuckle floats,
An acorn drops with a soft thud,
The woodland critters write their notes,
In this wacky, whimsical mud.

In cracks of bark, there's mirth on tap,
As jokes hang low, ripe for the pluck,
But who will gather them from the gap?
That stumped grin's the jester's luck!

Dappled Fragments of Joy

Sunbeams play hide and seek with the pines,
As shadows ripple like spilled ink,
A chipmunk jests, to the deer he's blind,
While crickets pause and think.

With twinkling eyes and a clumsy dance,
The branches sway in a leafy jest,
A goose in a hat might take a chance,
To impress a passing nest.

The echo of laughter sways with the breeze,
Yet tickles of mirth get lost in the leaves,
Where gnarled roots hide behind the trees,
And reason plays tricks with the eaves.

Oh, dappled fragments, so fleetingly bright,
Remind us that joy, like sunlight, is fleet,
Yet still in those moments, a spark of delight,
Glimmers faintly, a crumb, not quite sweet.

Chortles Beneath the Evergreens

Underneath where the tall ones sway,
A giggle of shadows dart and tease,
The fawns lend a hand in their playful way,
While nutty ambitions flutter with ease.

Frogs croak a tune, oh what a croon,
While whispers of jest scatter alight,
As fireflies gather, their tails in tune,
The night chuckles softly, delighting in night.

Through tangled vines, the laughter creaks,
As pine needles drop like jokes unspoken,
Birds hide their grins, with secrets to keep,
While the old trees murmur, eternally broken.

In this woodlands' theatre, absurdly bright,
The slapstick comedy plays on and on,
Yet the laughs just skip, like stones from a height,
Leaving traces of joy, now forever gone.

Hushed Whispers of Merriment

In twilight's hush, soft giggles wane,
Where the branches curl and sway,
A hedgehog pricks up, no longer mundane,
In this muted, whimsical ballet.

Leaves flutter down with a gentle tease,
Each rustle shows life's tender plight,
But amidst this calm, a spirit frees,
To twirl on the path, a delicate light.

Behind the thicket, a raccoon grins,
As he juggles acorns, just for fun,
While owls keep watch, with their lazy spins,
The echoes flicker, one by one.

Whispers of joy wrapped in the bark,
Flit like shadows, just out of reach,
Yet, who will remember the spark,
In a world that seems only to teach?

Subdued Chuckles in the Canopy

In the shade where shadows dance,
Squirrels plot their silly prance,
Branches sway with soft delight,
While puns bloom in fleeting light.

Beneath the boughs, a giggle stirs,
As birds exchange their friendly slurs,
The air is thick with muffled cheer,
A riddle waits for ears to hear.

Rustles rise like whispers bold,
As secrets of the leaves unfold,
Nature's jesters, wild and free,
Create a raucous symphony.

Though laughter drifts like autumn breeze,
It fills the woods with gentle tease,
In silence where the shadows play,
The mirth of greens will find a way.

From Roars to Whispers in the Woods.

Once, a lion's laugh would roar,
Now whispers flit from floor to floor,
The trees have tales of lightly tossed,
   A journey where the fun is lost.

A croak of frogs in twilight's haze,
Outshines the lion's mighty phrase,
With playful nudges, nature bends,
Where echoes bounce and laughter ends.

Mice in meetings share their schemes,
Beneath the moonlight's silver beams,
The darkened woods recall the sound,
   Of grins and giggles all around.

Yet in the silence of the trees,
Lies memories that still can tease,
A tinkle here, a chuckle there,
In every breeze, a hidden flare.

Whispers in the Woods

Among the trunks, the whispers rise,
With secrets spun beneath the skies,
A fox grins wide, his eyes aglow,
While shadows hide a playful show.

Tiny voices craft a joke,
That climbs with every steady poke,
A rustle hints at fun in flight,
As branches sway with soft delight.

Beneath the cone of verdant trees,
A symphony of chuckles tease,
Each twig unfurls a witty pun,
As golden rays weave through the fun.

In every nook, the laughter glows,
As frolic flows where nobody goes,
The greens embrace the playful jest,
In whispered tales, the woods are best.

Echoes of Forgotten Joy

In corners where the shadows creep,
Reside the echoes soft and deep,
Of laughter once that filled the air,
And dreams spun lightly everywhere.

The trees remember every grin,
Each chuckle that has ever been,
Yet now they sway in solemn pose,
Holding fast to what nobody knows.

A laughter trail once bright and clear,
Now hides in whispers, faint but near,
As sunlight flees and dusk arrives,
The ghosts of mirth in silence thrive.

But still beneath the branches wide,
A joke may stir the heart inside,
For even lost, those joys remain,
In windswept sighs, a sweet refrain.

Whirlwinds of Mirthful Memories

In the breeze, a ticklish tease,
Whispers of joy float with ease.
A squirrel wears a tiny hat,
Chasing shadows, imagine that!

Under the branches, laughter spryly dances,
Where giggles spark in sunny glances.
A chipmunk juggles acorns with flair,
While we share a knowing stare.

A prankster crow steals a pine cone,
We laugh and sigh, never alone.
The trees sway gently, in their glee,
Old memories wrapped in harmony.

So here we stand, with hearts so bright,
In love with nature's silly plight.
With every chuckle, two sparks ignite,
Turning the day into pure delight.

Muted Exclaims of Laughter's Loss

In the hush of woods, secrets dwell,
Quiet chuckles that we can't tell.
A fog rolls in, soft as a sigh,
Where giggles vanish, passing by.

Meandering paths where smiles fade,
Memories tucked in sunlight's shade.
A tree stump grins, holding the past,
Yet echoes linger, fading fast.

Soft whispers haunt, in the quiet space,
Where joy once bloomed, now leaves a trace.
A bunny hops, with a curious glance,
While shadows speak of our lost chance.

Yet in this gloom, hope takes root,
As laughter shines in the absolute.
Between the leaves, a secret spark,
Reminds us of joy, hidden but stark.

The Weaving of Whimsy's Shadow

Threads of giggles spin in the air,
Weaving joy everywhere.
With silly tales, we dance and play,
Chasing shadows at the end of the day.

Frolicking foxes, a wild ballet,
Paint the dusk in a humorous way.
While fairy tales twist through the trees,
Echoes of laughter ride the breeze.

A deer prances, a dance so grand,
Caught in the humor of this land.
Whimsy clings like leaves to a bough,
Crafting delight from here to now.

Yet in this play, amid the cheer,
Whispers of giggles just out of ear.
We find the warmth of shared regret,
And in the dusk, no need to fret.

Chasing Elation in Dusk's Embrace

As the sun dips low, colors collide,
We run with shadows, nowhere to hide.
In twilight's glow, we break into song,
Our hearts are light, where we belong.

With each step, the world spins round,
Echoes of laughter in silence found.
A misfit frog leaps for a cheer,
While fireflies twinkle, drawing near.

The night unfolds with a ticklish breeze,
Swirling the leaves with playful ease.
Under the stars, we make a wish,
For giggles lost and a hearty swish.

As dusk enfolds our joyful chase,
Memories linger in dreams, embrace.
Together we chase through night's sweet phase,
Finding mirrors of laughter in dusk's haze.

The Last Chime of Happiness

Once there was a jester, bright,
His jingle made folks take flight.
But one day he slipped on a pie,
The fruit flew high, oh my, oh my!

The laughter echoed through the trees,
As squirrels giggled on the breeze.
With every tumble and every trip,
They shared a chuckle, a joyous blip.

Yet time grew shadowy and dim,
The jester's joy began to slim.
Where are the giggles? Where's the cheer?
Now silence lingers, lost in fear.

So here I sit, my heart in tune,
Recalling how we danced 'neath the moon.
In a world where laughter used to bloom,
Now whispers echo, a heart's heavy doom.

Chasing Smiles Beneath the Boughs

Underneath the branches sway,
We ran in circles, come what may.
Chasing shadows, creating mirth,
Yet what was found? A case of dearth.

The giggles played like leaves in flight,
But now they're hidden from our sight.
What caused the glee to drift away?
Did a breeze carry it, or did it stray?

Cracked jokes hang heavy in the air,
While memories flaunt their vacant stare.
Oh, how we danced, how we sang,
Now silence looms, where did we hang?

Beneath the boughs, we'd break and bend,
A tapestry of laughter, without end.
Yet in that space, the echoes wane,
A bittersweet tune like falling rain.

Unraveled Chuckles in the Forest

In the thicket, whispers grow,
Once a riot, now moving slow.
Twisted tales in the tangled vine,
Weaving a tapestry, a lost design.

Silly antics, a slip on greens,
Now just shadows, hidden scenes.
With every joke spun low and high,
Where did they vanish? Oh, we sigh.

Frisky fairies once took flight,
Now drift away, lost from sight.
Those snickers and cackles, where have they flown?
In the depths of the woods, we sit alone.

Chasing echoes of our own delight,
But alas, remains a quiet blight.
So here we ponder, clutching sighs,
As twilight whispers, laughter dies.

Elusive Smirks Amongst the Leaves

A band of friends from days of yore,
Packed with jokes, our laughter tore.
But now the sprightly steps have stilled,
Where joy once bloomed, the air is chilled.

Among the leaves, we tossed our wits,
Crafting moments, pulling hits.
Yet now we sit, lost in the mist,
Searching for smiles that we once kissed.

What trembles here within our rib?
The echoes fade—what a fib!
Once we gathered in endless glee,
Where, oh where, did enchantment flee?

With playful secrets, spun with skill,
Now hushed whispers linger still.
Amongst the boughs, the shadows creep,
Once   we laughed, now we just weep.

Canopies Overforgotten Jests

Beneath the trees, the whispers play,
Old chuckles drift, like leaves in sway.
A squirrel giggles, tails in a whirl,
Chasing its shadow in a leafy twirl.

Sunlight dances on forgotten lore,
As moonlit nights recall the uproar.
The branches creak with a mischievous glee,
As if they're sharing a joke with me.

Rusty jokes in the bark's embrace,
Twisted humor finds its place.
We laugh alone at the silence spent,
And wonder where all the laughter went.

Echoes of fun in the wood's deep heart,
A symphony of joy that won't depart.
In each rustle, the memories chime,
A tapestry woven in laughter and rhyme.

Zephyr's Touch on Faded Smiles

A breeze sweeps through with a gentle sigh,
Tickling the branches, oh so spry.
Old joyous whispers, now faint and meek,
Play peek-a-boo in a game they seek.

The shadows stretch in playful sprawls,
As laughter bounces off unseen walls.
A humor washed out, yet still it clings,
Like forgotten dreams of unsung kings.

With every rustle, a giggle's trace,
Lurking softly in this quiet space.
While sunlight winks through the verdant screen,
It's harder to find what once might have been.

Yet smiles remain, though they're faintly cast,
Woven in whispers of merriment past.
As the zephyr dances with soft embrace,
We catch a glimpse of a joy we chase.

Stolen Moments of Amusement

Time slips through in a playful spree,
Nibbled on by the cheeky spree.
Laughter, like fruit, hangs on the vine,
Yet we stand wondering, where's the punchline?

The chipmunks sing, a cacophonous tune,
While sunlight fades, a comical swoon.
Each snicker echoes like footsteps of glee,
Yet still we ponder, where joy used to be.

The grass grows wild with secrets untold,
And in its midst, we dare to be bold.
Cracks in the laughter are marked by the past,
But the joy we find is forever vast.

In every flicker, a moment we steal,
A glimpse of the fun that time can't repeal.
Through larches and laughter, a path we still roam,
In stolen moments, we call laughter home.

The Weight of Lost Wit

In the boughs of yore, a riddle hangs,
Where laughter once danced, potential bangs.
The air is thick with memories' weight,
As echoes of humor whisper their fate.

Witty banter lost in the folds,
The stories wrap up like unturned molds.
In silence, we sift through the dusty remains,
Wishing to find the humor in chains.

Tickling fancies sneak past our eyes,
While shadows dance in forgotten ties.
Yet laughter through leaves may still be found,
In every creak, a new joke's sound.

Oh, the burden of tales left untold,
Mirth in the air is worth more than gold.
As we trudge through these woods of despair,
Let's lift up our hearts, let's lighten the air.

The Stillness After Joy's Departure

In the quiet of dusk, shadows play,
Whispers of chuckles, they fade away.
The tickles of moments spent in glee,
Now echo softly, like leaves on a tree.

A jester once pranced with a grin so wide,
Now the pebbles just sit by the side.
The frolic of brief, once lively and grand,
Now just a memory, hard to understand.

With each vacant space, a giggle hangs low,
Like a balloon that forgot how to glow.
Fond recollections in each rustling sound,
Chasing the joy that is nowhere around.

Yet in this stillness, a chuckle erupts,
From the heart as it playfully busts.
Mirth may have slipped, but it cannot delete,
The rhythm of joy that will always repeat.

Where Laughter Once Danced

In the sunlit glade, where joy had its say,
Now only the breeze comes out to play.
The echoes of laughter, a sweet serenade,
Now shadowed by silence, gently portrayed.

Where once there were antics, mirthful and bright,
Now the crickets take turns in the night.
A twirl of chortles, a jig on the grass,
Turns into whispers of moments gone past.

Each twig bears a story, a jest in the air,
But now they are hushed, too timid to share.
Squirrels seem sobered, no prance in their tails,
As if they remember those glorious tales.

Yet laughter still lingers, in corners unseen,
A flicker of joy, where it once had been.
Though the dance has paused, the spirit remains,
In the heart's quiet rhythm, the joy still remains.

The Residue of Merriment's Trail

Amidst the tall pines where fun used to roam,
A scent of sweet folly drifts back home.
The paths still remember the joy that we shared,
Though time has extinguished the laughter we dared.

With every soft breeze, a joyride appears,
But quickly subsides, replaced by our fears.
The lingering chuckles now fade like the stars,
Leaving soft shadows, old jokes with old scars.

While critters scurry, in playful delight,
They dip in the shadows and out of the light.
Yet whispers of giggles still rustle the leaves,
Reminding us gently of all that one leaves.

In the warmth of the sun, a remnant remains,
A sprinkle of joy amidst life's little pains.
Though moments grow quiet and laughter moves on,
The trail of our merriment lingers till dawn.

Heartbeats of Happiness Left Behind

In the corners of rooms, where smiles used to bloom,
The air hangs thick with a humorous gloom.
A flicker of joy, only ghosts do recall,
As if laughter's heartbeat has answered the call.

Tickles and giggles, once rang through the halls,
Now only the echo of silence befalls.
The chairs stand in rows like jesters in line,
Awaiting the punchline that's lost with the time.

The echoes of fun, like leaves on the breeze,
Migrate and flutter like stories from trees.
A wink in the shadows, a chuckle's embrace,
Leave traces of joy in an empty space.

Yet even in quiet, the heart finds a beat,
In memories wrapped in a warm, cozy seat.
So here's to the laughter, the moments we find,
In heartbeats of happiness left far behind.

The Forgotten Festival of Cheer

Once we danced in fields so wide,
Where jests and giggles never died.
Now the banners hang in dust,
And are whispers of what we trust.

Mirth made way for muted sighs,
As clowns don't juggle, truth belies.
The pies are stale and laughs grew thin,
Where did the joy of jest begin?

Remember when we'd race by trees,
With ticklish breezes 'neath the leaves?
Now shadows linger, filled with doubt,
The echoes of fun have faded out.

Oh, to hear a chuckle clear,
A trumpet blare of boisterous cheer!
But in silence now we wander slow,
To find that festival long ago.

Pauses in the Symphony of Smiles

A tune once played on merry days,
Now halts, it seems, in cloudy haze.
The piano's keys grow cold and gray,
While laughter fades, it slips away.

A jester's cap, once bright with jive,
Now sits untouched, where jests arrive.
The audience has left the scene,
Yet echoes of joy still intervene.

Each tick of time, a silent tease,
Where once we rallied with such ease.
Now moments pause, like stifled breath,
As smiles shrink deep, caught in the net.

But still, we search for sounds of glee,
In whispered winds, a memory.
The music waits, it longs to play,
For the symphony won't fade away.

Laughter's Erosion Over Time

Once we rolled on grassy hills,
With belly laughs and fleeting thrills.
But time has worn those echoes thin,
And rusted joy, where joy's been.

Laughter dripped from every tongue,
Now trickles softly, never sung.
Where are the jokes that lit the night?
They're ghosts now, dimmed by fading light.

Faces wore smiles, like painted art,
But now the frames just fall apart.
Once filled with hues of bright delight,
Now shadows linger, lost from sight.

Yet still, we fish in seas of sighs,
For hints of laughter, distant cries.
In every creak and whispered chime,
We seek the spark of bygone time.

Strings of Elation Dispersed

The strings of joy once strummed so high,
Now dangle low, beneath the sky.
They quivered with the grace of song,
Now the notes have drifted wrong.

A puppet show that lost its sheen,
With tangled cords and heads that lean.
The audience, a ghostly mist,
Where happiness no longer tryst.

Each string a memory, frayed and torn,
Of laughter shared, of spirits worn.
But every tear, a stitch of grace,
For woven tales leave softest trace.

Yet hope, it weaves a thread so fine,
That binds the heart and with it, shine.
So let us strum, though weak the hands,
For laughter lives where joy still stands.

Sunlit Grins and Gloomy Pines

In the shadow of tall trees, we played,
Every grin a secret, every laugh delayed.
Sunlight danced on leaves, a playful tease,
Yet echoes of chuckles drifted with ease.

Beneath the boughs, our giggles grew,
Strange sounds emerged, but none we knew.
Pines whispered tales of jokes long forgot,
While our silly antics ran wild in the plot.

Silly stumbles on pinecone-strewn trails,
Our joyful mischief told humorous tales.
But the grumpy old trees just stood and stared,
As our laughter fluttered, light and unpaired.

Days stretched like shadows, warmth in retreat,
With every snicker, we felt bittersweet.
For nature's embrace, though solemn and grand,
Could not hold the joy we let slip from hand.

The Traces of Unshared Jokes

Whispers of wit flit between the leaves,
With every snort, the larch just grieves.
We shared our punchlines, the trees grew still,
Their branches drooped, lost all sense of thrill.

In our private world, humor was bright,
But with each shared laugh, shadows grew slight.
Giddy moments that bloomed in the air,
Faded like whispers, unsure we were there.

Footsteps echoed on the forest floor,
As our laughter bounced off the larch's door.
Yet treetops sighed, black clouds in the sky,
Holding onto jokes we could never deny.

Silent soon came, the sun dipped low,
Memories lingered but felt like a show.
Where once was merriment, a quiet sigh,
The traces of laughter ever passing by.

Mournful Echoes of Lively Days

In fields where we tumbled, the sun on our face,
Now lays a silence, a curious space.
Once vibrant and full, our laughter rang clear,
Now faint echoes whisper, "Where did they steer?"

The larch stands tall, like a watchful friend,
Yet cradles our chuckles that seem to descend.
Broken are moments once lively and bright,
As shadows now linger, consuming the light.

Had those carefree times taken flight with the breeze?
Left only murmurs, our soft melodies.
With each memory pinned, like a butterfly,
Life's comic adventures start to say goodbye.

Caught in the dance between joy and despair,
The forest remembers, although we are rare.
And still it stands there—bitter, yet sweet,
Keeping our secrets in laughter's defeat.

Memories That Flee Like Shadows

Under the canopy, we once found delight,
Jokes spun like webs, capturing the light.
Each muffled chuckle, in whispers would spread,
Now memories flee like shadows, long fled.

The trees keep the tales of our folly and fun,
Their arms are now empty where laughter was spun.
In every rustle, a hint of the past,
Yet moments of mirth just never held fast.

Starlit giggles beneath swaying pines,
Elusive echoes like tangled designs.
We chased the joy that slipped through our hands,
An amusing mirage in shifting sands.

The sun dips low, and we pause in time,
With every smile, just a mountain to climb.
Though shadows may gather, the heart knows no fear,
For laughter once lived, and its spirit is near.

Echoing Chuckles Beneath the Trees

In the shade where shadows play,
A squirrel danced, then ran away.
A rabbit tripped on roots so sly,
And giggles echoed, oh my my!

The wind would tease with rustling leaves,
Whispers played tricks, oh how it weaves.
An owl blinked, with a bemused stare,
While bunnies bounced without a care.

Chipmunks plotting mischief grand,
With acorn hats, their own command.
A chorus of chirps, such a delight,
As laughter warmed the chilly night.

In this wood, such mirth held dear,
Moments of joy, we hold them near.
As echoes fade and time creeps on,
We cherish fun 'til it is gone.

Fragments of Glee in the Forest

Beneath the boughs, a jester's cheer,
Where laughter bubbled, crystal clear.
A bear wore shades, quite a sight,
While birds exchanged jokes taking flight.

The brook chuckled with every splash,
As time slipped by in a playful dash.
A fox recited a comedic rhyme,
While shadows danced, mocking time.

Mushrooms sprouting like little hats,
Joined the fray with the furry chaps.
A wind-up snail raced, oh so slow,
While fireflies winked in the twilight glow.

Yet as the sun began to fall,
The laughter faded, a gentle call.
We gathered memories, tucked them in tight,
As echoes of joy slipped into night.

The Amusement That Slipped Away

In a glen where giggles roam,
A raccoon tried to find a home.
With sticky paws and a grand display,
He flopped and flailed in disarray.

A fox, adorned in a muted vest,
Slyly planned a comedic jest.
With puns that floated on sweet breeze,
He tickled the fawns, brought them to knees.

But time's a thief, it crept and stole,
The merry warmth from every soul.
As shadows stretched and laughter fled,
We waved goodbye to joy instead.

Yet in the heart of every glade,
The fragments of fun will never fade.
In whispered winds, the echoes play,
Reminding us of our brighter day.

Woodland Whimsy and Whispers

In the woods where the breezes giggle,
A hedgehog wobbled, quite a wiggle.
With prickle and poke, he played a prank,
On rabbits hiding in the bank.

A troupe of frogs sang songs of cheer,
While crickets joined, 'twas music clear.
With every ribbit, a chuckle pops,
As nature's laughter never stops.

But as dusk blankets the land,
Whispers flutter like grains of sand.
The mirth retreats, a shy goodbye,
As stars twinkle in the velvet sky.

Yet memories linger, sweet like dew,
In every rustle, in every view.
For laughter lives in memory's grasp,
In all the woods where joy does clasp.

www.ingramcontent.com/pod-product-compliance
Lightning Source LLC
Chambersburg PA
CBHW071848160426
43209CB00003B/466